amicus
illustrated

MATH WORLD
TELLING
TIME

BY BRIDGET HEOS   ILLUSTRATED BY KATYA LONGHI

Amicus Illustrated is published by Amicus
P.O. Box 1329, Mankato, MN 56002
www.amicuspublishing.us

Editor: Rebecca Glaser
Designer: Kathleen Petelinsek

Library of Congress Cataloging-in-Publication Data
Heos, Bridget, author.
 Telling time / by Bridget Heos ; illustrated by Katya Longhi.
    pages cm. — (Math world)
 Summary: "A young boy learns to tell time on digital and
analog clocks as he impatiently waits for a friend to come
over to play." — Provided by publisher.
 Audience: K to grade 3.
 Includes index.
 ISBN 978-1-60753-461-7 (library binding) —
ISBN 978-1-60753-676-5 (ebook)
1. Time—Juvenile literature. 2. Clocks and watches—Juvenile
literature. I. Longhi, Katya, illustrator. II. Title.
 QB209.5.H46 2015
 529.7—dc23   2013034685

Printed in the United States of America at Corporate Graphics
in North Mankato, Minnesota.

10 9 8 7 6 5 4 3 2 1

ABOUT THE AUTHOR

Bridget Heos is the author of more than
60 books for kids and teens, including many
books for Amicus Illustrated and her recent
picture book *Mustache Baby* (Houghton
Mifflin Harcourt, 2013). She lives in Kansas City
with her husband and four children. Visit her
on the Web at www.authorbridgetheos.com.

ABOUT THE ILLUSTRATOR

Katya Longhi was born in southern Italy. She
studied illustration at the Nemo NT Academy
of Digital Arts in Florence. She loves to create
dream worlds in her illustrations. She currently
lives in northern Italy with her Prince Charming.

"What's the matter, James?"

"Mia, please, call me Ninja."

"What's the matter...Ninja?"

"Antonio is coming over at 10:00 to play ninjas."

"That sounds like fun."

"But, Mia, I don't know when he's coming. I can't tell time!"

"I'll teach you."

"The number to the left of the dots, or colon, tells the hour. It's 9 something.

The numbers to the right of the dots tell the minutes. No minutes have passed.

It's exactly 9 o'clock. Have you eaten breakfast, James, I mean Ninja?"

"No," says James. "I'm hungry."
"Look, the clock changed. :01 means that one minute has passed."

"And now it is 9:02?"
"Right, Ninja!"

"What time is it now?" Mia asks.

"It's one after nine again! A bad ninja must be moving the clock backwards," James says.

"No, James, it's 9:10. Ten minutes have passed since 9:00. There are 60 minutes in an hour. You have 50 minutes to wait."

"Why are you so slow, clock?"

"We could try a different clock. What if instead of a digital clock, you have an analog clock, like this? Don't worry, James. You can tell time this way, too."

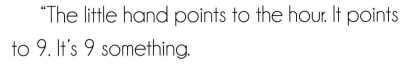

"The little hand points to the hour. It points to 9. It's 9 something.

Pretend your finger is the little hand. Move it from one to twelve around the clock."

"The big hand points to the minutes. It points to 2."

"So is it 9:02 again?"

"Not quite, James. For the big hand, each number stands for five minutes. So if you count by fives, it's 9:10 right now."

"Oh, I think I get it, Mia! 9:05, 9:10, 9:15, 9:20..."

"If only time moved as fast as you can count, Antonio would already be here!"

"But a little time has passed, right Mia?"

"Right. Now, it's 9:15. Isn't watching the clock fun?"

"Not really. Can we play ninjas now?"

"All right, ninja James. But stay close to the clock. Something big is going to happen, and you won't want to miss it."

"Hey, the clock hands sort of look like ninja swords."

"It's 9:30!"

"Wait, Mia. What's so great about 9:30?"

"Well, the clock chimes. And thirty minutes make half an hour. You're halfway to when Antonio comes."

"Let's see, what could
we do for half an hour?
We could:
Watch one T.V. show.
Walk the dog.
Make rice crispy treats.
Or shoot 60 baskets."

"So now you know how to tell time, James. Is it 10:00 yet?"

"The little hand points to the 10. So it's 10 something."

"And the big hand points to the 12. That means zero minutes have passed. It is exactly 10:00."

"Hi, Antonio!"

"I'll pick you up at 12:00,"
says Antonio's mom.

"But I can't tell time, mom,"
says Antonio.

"I'll teach you how, Antonio,"
says James.

READ MORE

Cleary, Brian P. A Second, a Minute, a Week with Days in It: A Book about Time. Minneapolis: Millbrook Press, 2013.

Harris, Trudy and Carrie Hartman. **The Clock Struck One: A Time-telling Tale.** Minneapolis: Millbrook Press, 2009.

Loughran, Donna. Time Ticks By: How Do You Read a Clock? Chicago: Norwood House Press, 2013.

Rosa-Medoza, Gladys. **What Time Is It?** New York: Windmill Books, 2011.

WEBSITES

ABCya! Learn to Tell Time
http://www.abcya.com/telling_time.htm
Drag hands on an analog clock or change numbers on a digital clock to practice telling time in this game with four levels of difficulty.

Stop the Clock
http://www.oswego.org/ocsd-web/games/StopTheClock/sthec1.html
Time yourself as you match the digital and analog clocks.

A Walk through Time
http://www.nist.gov/pml/general/time/index.cfm
Learn the history of telling time and different clocks people have used.

Every effort has been made to ensure that these websites are appropriate for children. However, because of the nature of the Internet, it is impossible to guarantee that these sites will remain active indefinitely or that their contents will not be altered.